Part of the Little Scientists Series

Where Do Babies Come From?

By Esmond Cooper

Both are important. One person can't make a baby alone.

They're different, but they both help make a baby.

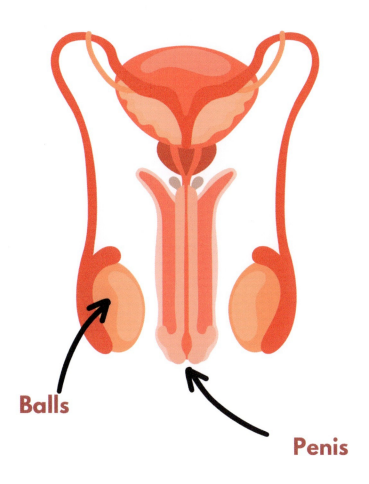

The man has balls.

Inside these balls are tiny tadpole-like things. People call them sperm.

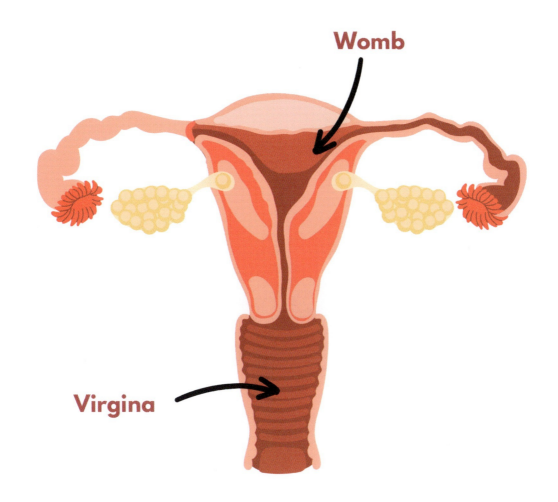

The woman has a special place in her body. It's not her tummy where food goes. It's a special womb.

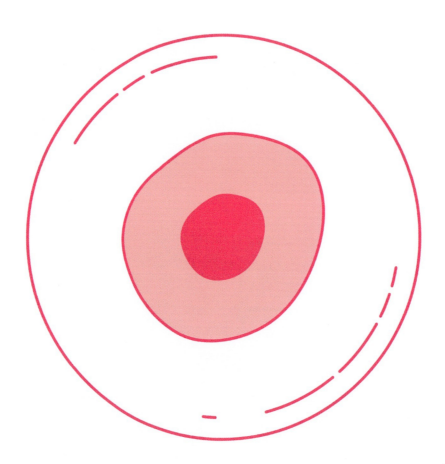

Inside the womb, there's a tiny, soft egg.

Sometimes when grown-ups love each other, they decide to have a baby.

The man and the woman get close.

They hug and kiss. This is having sex. This isn't just for making babies; it's a way grown-ups show love.

During this, the sperm swims out from the man and goes into the woman's body.

Think of it as a race. All the sperm swim super fast. They want to reach the egg first.

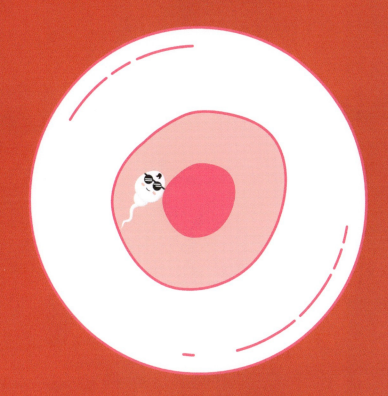

One sperm wins the race. It joins the egg.

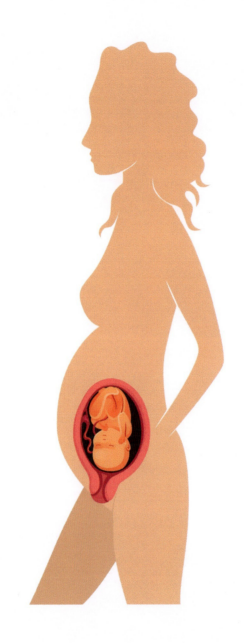

Something special starts to happen. A baby begins to grow inside the woman's special place, the womb.

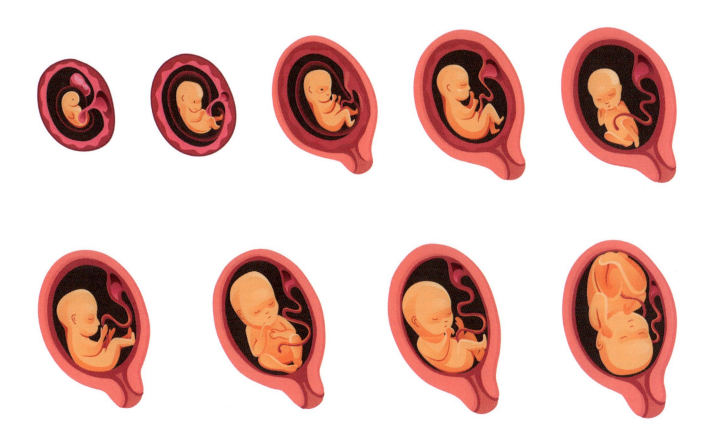

At first, you're tiny. But day by day, you grow bigger. Mom feels it. Her belly starts to get bigger too.

Mom feels it. Her belly starts to get bigger too.

A scan at the hospital can show if the baby is a girl or a boy. Mom and Dad can learn this before the baby is born.

After about nine months, it's time for the baby to come out.

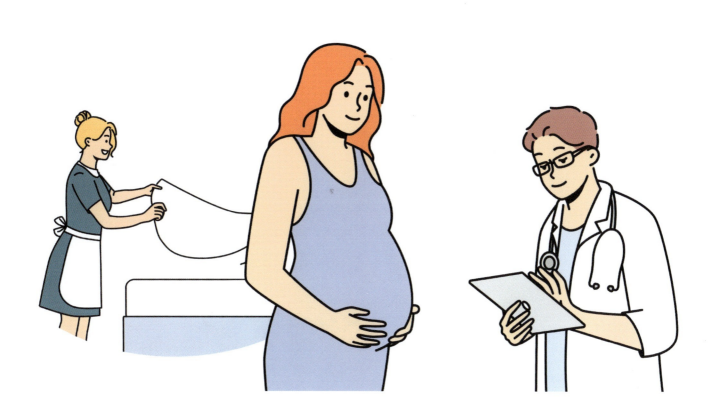

Mom goes to the hospital. People there, like doctors and nurses, help a lot. They help Mom.

They help Mom. They help the baby come out.

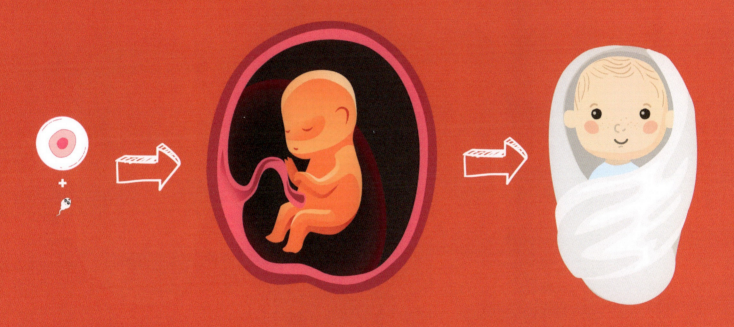

You started as a tiny sperm and a tiny egg. They met, joined, and you began to grow. Then you came out into the world and joined a family.

END

Where Do Babies Come From?

1. This is a woman. This is a man.
2. Both are important. One person can't make a baby alone.
3. They're different, but they both help make a baby.
4. The man has balls.
5. Inside these balls are tiny tadpole-like things. People call them sperm.
6. The woman has a special place in her body. It's not her tummy where food goes. It's a special womb.
7. Inside the womb, there's a tiny, soft egg.
8. Sometimes when grown-ups love each other, they decide to have a baby.
9. The man and the woman get close.
10. They hug and kiss. This is having sex. This isn't just for making babies; it's a way grown-ups show love.
11. During this, the sperm swim out from the man and go into the woman's body.
12. Think of it as a race. All the sperm swim super fast. They want to reach the egg first.
13. One sperm wins the race. It joins the egg.
14. Something special starts to happen. A baby begins to grow inside the woman's special place, the womb.
15. At first, you're tiny. But day by day, you grow bigger. Mom feels it. Her belly starts to get bigger too.
16. Mom feels it. Her belly starts to get bigger too.
17. A scan at the hospital can show if the baby is a girl or a boy. Mom and Dad can learn this before the baby is born.
18. After about nine months, it's time for the baby to come out.
19. Mom goes a hospital. People there, like doctors and nurses, help a lot. They help Mom. They help the baby come out.
20. They help Mom. They help the baby come out.
21. You started as a tiny sperm and a tiny egg. They met, joined, and you began to grow. Then you came out into the world and joined a family.
22. End.